Young's Delight

Quarterly Magazine for the youths

Editor: Jane Austin

Tatiana Khabarova,

Jonathan Emmanuel

Published by Brims World

Printed in U.S.A.

ISBN: 9798664493481

CONTENTS

PREFACE

Welcome back! It is nice to get your attention again through our all consuming magazine. In this series, we have all it takes to fill you with more knowledge on how to live a comfortable youthful life. Growing up is not as easy as anyone thinks especially for those who have passed through it. The furnace could be either bearable or unbearable for such ones. Homes for the youths could be a thing of deceit where many display different attitude and another to who they are in the public eyes. Some youths are well behaved at home while outside people eye them differently. A good name should be chosen not a name that defiles. Keep on doing what is right in the sight of your family and people around you. Keep a good name!

Read on and enjoy!

Jane Austin

Publishing editor

YOUR AGE

Pieces of Advice for You

In order to maintain your youth, there are many ideas to put into consideration. The following will be valuable to you.

a) Enjoy your youth.

b) Take one step at a time.

c) Maintain good moral.

d) Have courage.

e) Do not be anxious.

f) Do not neglect help from others.

g) Be positive.

h) Embrace success.

i) Aim high.

j) Maintain good company.

RECIPE FOR YOU

HOW TO MAKE SPAGHETTI SQUASH

Ingredients

1 Spaghetti Squash (about 3 pounds) 2 Tablespoons Olive Oil, divided 1 small Onion, chopped

3 Cloves Garlic , crushed or finely minced 1 pound un-cooked Italian Sausage 1 Tablespoon finely chopped fresh Oregano (or 1 teaspoon dried oregano) - or whichever preferred herb 1 cup grated Parmesan cheese Kosher Salt or Sea Salt , to taste.

Cook it!

Different ways to cook spaghetti squash.

- **How to Cook Spaghetti Squash   in the Slow Cooker**

- Scrub squash clean and carefully pierce all over with a knife

(10-15 cuts, 1/2-inch to 1-inch in size).

- Place squash in slow cooker and place the cover on. Carefully remove squash and let cool slightly. Use a fork to separate the squash into strands.

How to cook a whole spaghetti in the microwave.

- Cooking Spaghetti Squash in the Microwave. Once the squash is cut in half and you've scooped out the seeds, just flip it upside down in a baking dish, fill it with about an inch of water, and microwave until soft.

- This usually takes another five to 10 minutes, depending on the size of the squash and your microwave.

How to bake spaghetti squash in the oven.

- Split the squash in half and scrape out seeds. Line an oven tray with aluminum foil. Season the spaghetti squash with olive oil, salt, and pepper. Place flesh side down and roast for 30 to 40 minutes until fully cooked.

If 40 minutes have passed, and you are not sure if the squash is ready, pull it out of the oven and drag the tines of a fork on the cut side. If spaghetti-like strands easily release from the skin, it's ready. If not,

continue baking and check on it every 5 to 10 minutes.

Over-roasting can lead to soggier "spaghetti", so it's best to keep a close eye on the squash.

Shred it.

When it's ready, leave it to cool slightly before creating "spaghetti" with your fork.

Shred it more to bring out the spagetti.

You can mix it up with ingredients.

Serve it!

You can add spagetti sorce and meat.

You can serve it with vegetables.

MORAL   Respect   **Courtesy**

Consideration   Decency   Propriety

Honesty   Uprightness

MORAL

Moral values should be held in high esteem. The young ones need to understand how to put into practice the following: respect, courtesy, consideration, decency, propriety, honesty and uprightness. They must have enough self-discipline

to hold up to these values.

Respect

This is the act of honoring someone by exhibiting care, concern, or consideration for their needs or feelings.

Synonyms: Esteem, regard, high, regard, high, opinion, acclaim, admiration, approbation, approval, appreciation, estimation, favor, popularity, recognition, veneration, awe, reverence, deference, honor, praise, homage, due regard, consideration, thoughtfulness, attentiveness, politeness, courtesy, civility, etc.

Courtesy

This is one way of showing politeness in one's attitude and behavior toward others.

Synonyms: politeness, grace, good manners, civility, gallantry.

Consideration

This is a thoughtful or sympathetic regard or respect; thoughtfulness for others:

Synonyms: Thought, deliberation, reflection,

contemplation, cogitation, rumination, pondering, meditation, musing, mulling, examination, inspection.

Decency

It is a strong sense of right and wrong, and a high standard of honesty, etc.

Synonyms: Propriety, decorum, seemliness, good taste, respectability, dignity, correctness, good form, etiquette, appropriateness, appropriacy, etc.

Propriety

This is conformity to what is socially acceptable in conduct or speech.

Synonyms: Decorum, respectability, decency, correctness, appropriateness, good manners, courtesy, politeness, rectitude, civility, modesty, etc.

Honesty

It is when you speak the truth and act truthfully.

Synonyms: Moral correctness, uprightness, honorableness, honor, integrity, morals, morality, ethics, principle, etc.

Uprightness

It is conduct that conforms to an accepted standard of right and wrong.

Synonyms: Rectitude, decency integrity principle honesty honor honorableness, respectability, high-mindedness, etc.

POETRY

FLYING HIGH

Flying high is what I want

Nothing can pull me down

I am all that matters

So do not make me give up!

Flying high is what I want

Looking down will not be it

I am holding on to it

So give me a chance!

Flying high is what I want

When all in bliss become

And my wish accomplished

So up above the sky ! hover!

YOUNG MOVIES

Sleep over

Comedy 2004

It is an American comedy where four girls with one of them having a party and they end up having the adventure of their lives....

Save The Last Dance
1 & 2
2001 & 2006

A promising dancer named Sara Johnson lost her mum in a tragic accident while coming for her audition. She moved in with her estranged father and transferred to an inner-city college. ....

It's a boy girl thing

Movie 2006

Pretty teen girl Neil is extremely bookish and can't wait to move on to higher education while her neighbor and classmate, Woody wants just to play football...

Tarzan

Movie 1999

Life of a small orphan named Tarzan who was raised by an ape named Kala....

My Young Auntie

Action and Adventure 1981

It is a comedy where a female martial-arts champion by name Cheng Tai-nun marries an elderly man......

CAREER

BECOMING AN ENGINEER

If you want to become an engineer these are the subjects to pass: Chemistry, physics, biology, algebra, geometry, trigonometry, pre-calculus and calculus. in most branches of engineering you must have good grades in math and science.

Types of Engineering

Mechanical engineering

This relates to the design and analysis of heat and mechanical power for the operation of machines and mechanical systems.

Civil engineering

It deals with the design, construction and maintenance of the physical and natural built environments.

Chemical engineering

This is the application of chemical, physical and biological sciences to the process of converting raw materials or chemicals into more useful or valuable forms.

Electrical engineering

This is the study and application of electricity, electronics and electro-magnetism.

Other engineering fields

Aerospace engineering

Aquaculture engineering,

Biomechanical engineering

Bioprocess engineering,

Biotechnical engineering

Ecological engineering,

Food engineering Forest engineering

Health and safety engineering

Natural resources engineering

Machinery systems engineering

Information and electrical systems engineering

Applied engineering

Biomedical engineering,

Biological engineering

Biosystems engineering

Biomedical engineering,

Building services engineering

Information engineering

Industrial engineering

Manufacturing engineering,

Component engineering,

Systems engineering,

Construction engineering,

Safety engineering,

Reliability engineering

Mechatronics engineering

Engineering management

Military engineering

Nanoengineering

Nuclear engineering

.Petroleum engineering

Project engineering

Railway engineering

Software engineering

Supply chain engineering

Cryptographic engineering

Information technology engineering or information engineering methodology

Web engineering

Systems engineering

Textile engineering

WORDS OF WISDOM

Wise words

Learn to be calm and you will always be happy.

Good things never came very easy.

Opportunity comes but once so grab it when it comes poking at you.

Once we believe in ourselves, the sky is the limit.

To think right you must think deep.

If you respect your elders you will eat with kings.

If you are not happy with what you have now how will you be happy with more.

When one door closes another opens.

It is nice to be important but more important to be nice.

COPING WITH YOUR SIBLINGS

We must recognize the importance of siblings. Our brothers and sisters are part of our lives; therefore they must be in our thoughts often.

1. **Make God your guide**

You must let God be in full control. Your family should embrace godliness which is the key to peaceful life.

2. Strong relationship

There must be strong relationship among all of you. This bond must reflect deep love and care no matter what condition you find yourselves.

3. **Accommodate each other**

Stick by one another despite all odds. Individuals do not have the same behavior. Siblings are different from one another and while they grow together, they must tolerate one another.

4. **Emphasize on the good**

Admonish one another even if it means covering up each other's weaknesses. Encourage your siblings and repeatedly mention the nice things they did.

5. **Grow together**

You must all focus your attention on growing together as one family. Do not let quarrels and differences destroy the bond. Let the bond stretch on to when you will have separate families in the future.

6. **Love one another**

Love is the greatest which must be evident and expressed among you all. When you are concerned about your siblings and vice versa, this is a sign of love in the family. Embrace it, reveal it and show it!

7. **Team work**

 Work together as a family. Divide the household chores among yourselves and them wholeheartedly. Do not leave decision making to your parents only, chip in some ideas too.

8. **Do not neglect**

When your sibling is having

a problem help out in any

way you can. Give

comforting words and be

around often. This action

could help ease tension

and give encouragement.

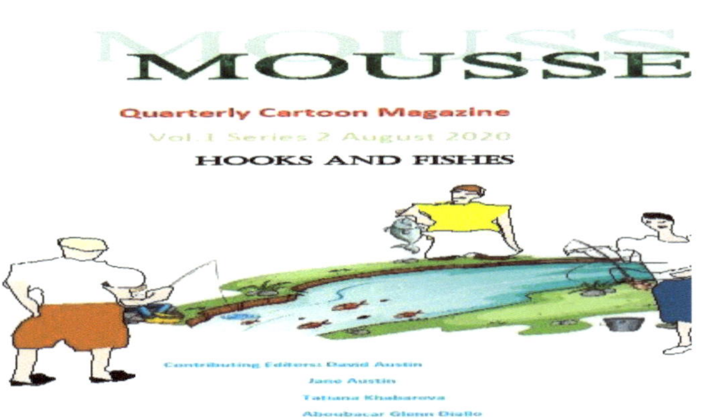

MOUSSE

Your favorite cartoon magazine is here! Purchase it online at amazon.com.

MAKING A GOOD GRADE

1. Motivation

There is a lot to do to get a good grade. You must put in enough effort through studying hard,. Motivation is your number one priority. Do not let anyone put you down. Always say I will try and make it.

2. Participation

Your contribution in the class will encourage your personality. It will show you are not left out and the effort will not be in vain. Always let your teachers know the areas you lack understanding. Moreover, will show you are interested in your studies.

3. Important notes

Writing out good points to remember while studying is very important. Some teachers are very fast and might not repeat what they said earlier. It is your right to write what you think is necessary to know. This will be bonus for you when you sit for the examination.

4. Concentration

It is important to concentrate fully in the class. Many students are distracted by other unserious ones. Do not listen to jokes made by them. Avoid leaving the class while lessons are going on. Do not daydream during lessons such as thinking about a friend you are visiting or an outfit you want to buy.

5. Do your homework

Homework carries some percentage to give you good grades. You must always do your homework correctly. Do not handle your homework lightly. Research and make enough findings that will fit into the answers for the questions you are tackling. Your presentation will determine your success. Well answered questions will earn high percentage.

6. Take a break

You do not need to sit all day long studying. You must take a break. Stretch yourself on the bed and relax. Do not watch movies or listen to music. Noise will not give you rest or break. The pictures your eyes are watching and the noise your ears are hearing will get you down. You can also

take a walk with your dog or alone. If you live close to the woods, take a walk round the woods and take pure air. It will cool your brain.

7. Be organized

Do not scatter your books round the room. Put different subjects separately so that you can reach for them without searching too long. Making effort to look for a book will reduce the energy to assimilate effectively.

8. Make a plan

Write out the dates for your tests and examinations. There are notebooks for jotting important things. You must frequently check your jotter to be reminded of the dates for your tests and examinations.

9. Reading schedule

You must have specified reading schedules. Draft out days and hours to read the subjects you are learning at school. Learning each subject at a good pace will give you room to assimilate and remember all you have studied.

10. Group study

It is noteworthy to understand that group study is important too. Peers coming together to study help one another in areas of weaknesses. They share ideas and work on problems that one person cannot deal with. Select days such as after school or weekends to meet and study.

Good Luck!

FOCUSING ON GOD

Jean Forde

Holding on to God's words can make a lot of difference in your life. How do you do this? The words of God tell you what to do in different situations. In order to know what is in the words of God you must have a complete bible.

The bible must contain both the old and new testaments. Every day you must read your bible and memorise some important portions that you can recite whenever you are in a difficult time.
The following passages in the bible help you to focus your attention on God, the Creator. Depending on God and having faith in Him through our Lord Jesus Christ will grant you assurance and peace of mind.

Salvation   Romans 10:13

Holy Spirit   Ephesians 1:13-14

Faith   Matthew 21:21-22

Thankful   Psalm 100

Fear   Luke 12:5

Courage   Psalm 27:14

God's protection   Psalm 91

Needing peace   John 14:27

Depressed   Psalm 34

Sick or pain   Isaiah 53: 3-7

CLOTHING

COPING WITH COLD

FOR BOTH MALE AND FEMALE.
KEEP WARM!

YOUNG MALE'S COLD WEARS

DON'T
STOP
Believin'
Thankfull

YOUR HEALTH

TATIANA KHABAROVA

How to Stay Healthy

1 Exercise regularly.

These are some very exciting exercises:

Swimming

Biking

Dancing

Playing tennis

Jogging

Yard work

2 Eat a healthy diet.

The following contain healthy diet

Vegetables

Fruits

Protein

Less carbohydrate

3 Maintain a healthy weight.

Observe the following to keep a healthy weight.

Have a good diet plan.

Regularly weigh yourself.

Daily exercise is good for you.

Do not depend on restaurant meals. Prepare your food.

4 Get enough sleep.

These are two types of
sleep for good health.

1-3 hours for siesta

7-9 hours of sleep per night

 5 **Do not listen to loud
music. This can damage
your hearing for the rest
of your life.**

SPORTS

BADMINTON

Badminton is played as a casual outdoor activity in a yard or on a beach. Most formal games are played on a rectangular indoor court. A player scores points when he strikes the shuttlecock with the racquet and it landed within the opposing side's half of the court. Each side ought to strike the shuttlecock one time before it passes over the net.

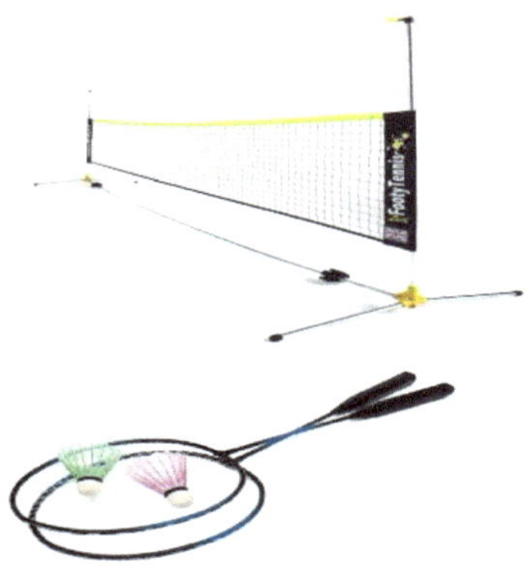

Badminton players need the following: a net, a shuttlecock, and at least two rackets. The net crosses the center of the badminton court.

Each player must all the time hit the center of the shuttlecock. He has to hit the round rubber centre of the shuttle every single time. Players practice this technique by looking right at the center of the shuttle when they hit an overhead shot. They can also practice with their hands in order to get a feel for the shuttle.

How to hit the shuttle at the top of its arc.

To benefit from the speed and height generated by the shuttle, hit it at the top of its arc. This will allow you to shoot a killer overhead and to have more control over the position of the shuttle. Don't wait for the shuttle to come close to you, or it will be losing momentum and height.

How to hit the shuttle toward the back line.

It takes precision and strength, to hit the shuttle toward the back line. This movement will make your opponent have to shuffle backwards and hit the shuttle with much strength to return your shot. If it is not clear where to hit the shuttle next, and the back line is wide open, aim it there. When the game starts, aim the shuttle a bit before the back line and it will not become an error if it falls out of bounds behind the back line.

Getting accustomed to your footwork

The footwork brings you good points when you can balance correctly as you play. Flat-footed players on the court cannot return shots. It is appropriate for a player to stay on his toes. He needs to move his feet up and down as he waits to return a shot, and move his feet back and forth and side to side in tiny motions to position himself to return the shot. He must reach out his hand wide enough to try to return the shuttle also make quick movements with your feet until the shuttle is in perfect position. Practicing helps a lot and a smart player will always make good points out of it.

Try it out and enjoy!

MUSIC

Singing

The vocal chords are made of muscle which ought to be stretched before you start singing. You can warm up in a variety of ways.

Practice your major scales, starting with the middle C, moving down in half-steps before moving up. Do not push yourself before you are actually singing, and try to move slowly. When you warm up constantly,
You will be able to articulate all the notes in the scales very well.

Breathing exercises

Breathing exercises helps beginners to control better the pitch and duration of their singing. Singers who can breathe deeply will always get better mileage out of their voice.

Practice opening your throat opening. Relax and open the jaw like a fish might out of water. Start flexing your facial muscles a little bit in between. Do this often and the result will be marvelous. Once you get your voice ready, you can compose a melodious song for listeners to appreciate and love!

GAMES

Tic-tac-toe or noughts and crosses. It is also referred to as Xs and Os.

It is a paper-and-pencil game for two players, *X* and *O*, who take turns marking the spaces in a 3×3 grid. The player who succeeds in placing three of their marks in a horizontal, vertical, or diagonal row is the winner.

The following example game is won by the first player, X:

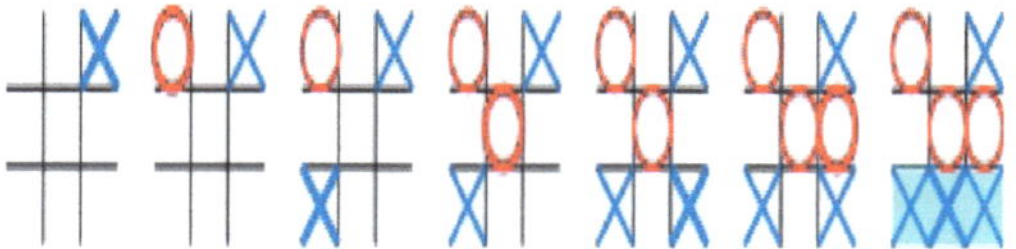

Tic-tac-toe

A completed game of Tic-tac-toe

Genre(s)	<u>Paper-and-pencil game</u>
Players	2
Setup time	Minimal
Playing time	~1 minute
Random chance	None
Skill(s) required	<u>Strategy</u>, tactics, observation

In order to win the game, a

player must place three in a

row, horizontal or vertical.

Try your luck! Write out your score.

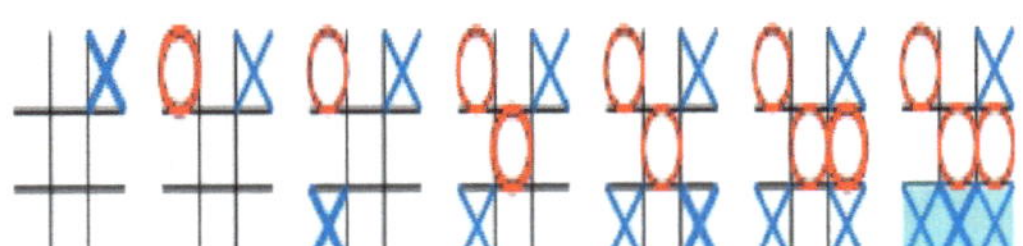

Cross word   Fill in the

blanks the listed words. Begin with the letter in the box.

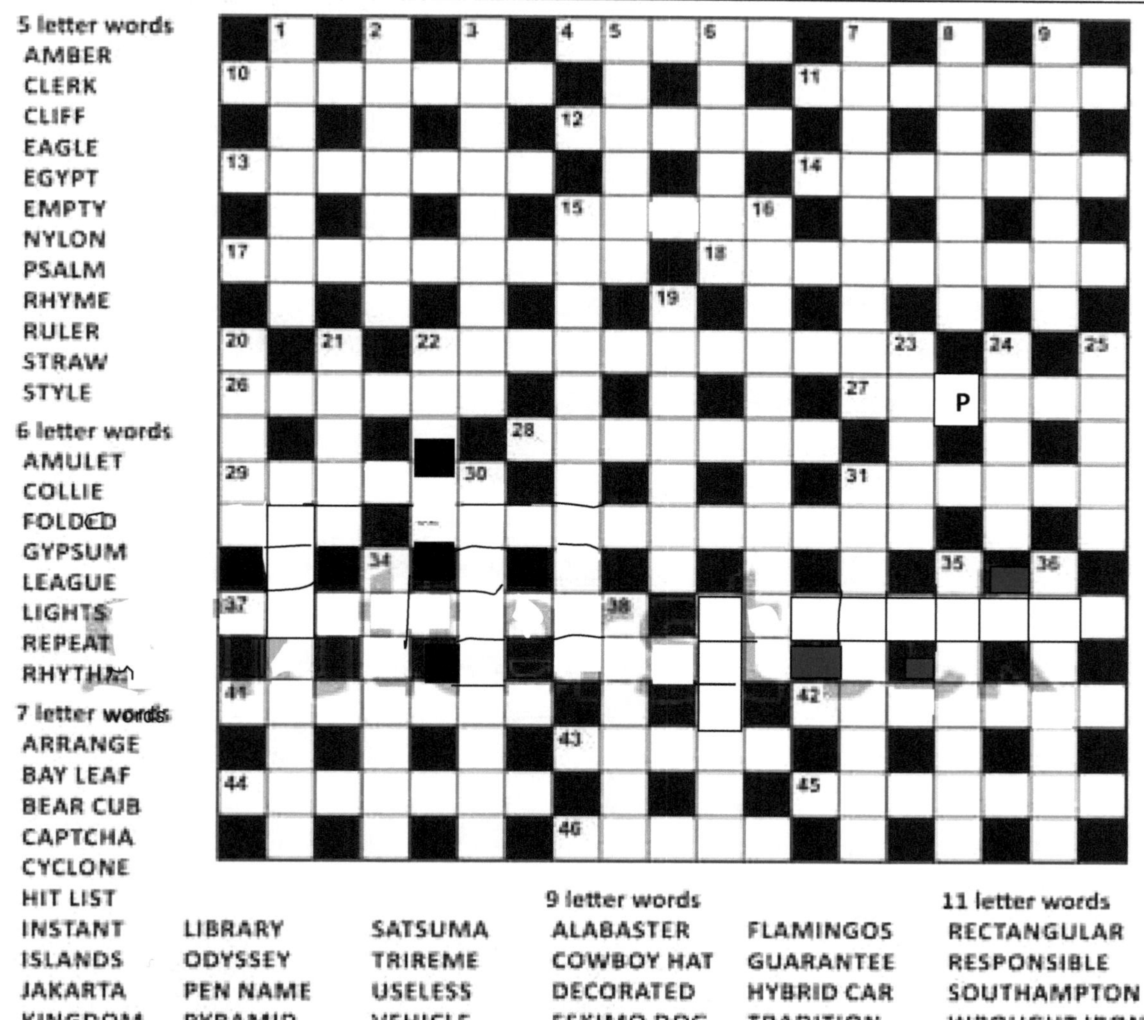

5 letter words
AMBER
CLERK
CLIFF
EAGLE
EGYPT
EMPTY
NYLON
PSALM
RHYME
RULER
STRAW
STYLE

6 letter words
AMULET
COLLIE
FOLDED
GYPSUM
LEAGUE
LIGHTS
REPEAT
RHYTHM

7 letter words
ARRANGE
BAY LEAF
BEAR CUB
CAPTCHA
CYCLONE
HIT LIST
INSTANT
ISLANDS
JAKARTA
KINGDOM

LIBRARY
ODYSSEY
PEN NAME
PYRAMID

SATSUMA
TRIREME
USELESS
VEHICLE

9 letter words
ALABASTER
COWBOY HAT
DECORATED
ESKIMO DOG

FLAMINGOS
GUARANTEE
HYBRID CAR
TRADITION

11 letter words
RECTANGULAR
RESPONSIBLE
SOUTHAMPTON
WROUGHT IRON

ADVICE CORNER BY NIKKY

Q. Hi, I am 18 years old male and I want to live away from my parents. Is it a good thing to do?

A. Are you already working? If not, you will not be able to afford to rent an apartment. Think about it and make sure you can afford it.

Q. I recently got a scholarship to go to a university. I do not want to leave my present job. What do I do? Continue my job or quite and go to the university.

A. Choosing a university with scholarship backing it up will upgrade your status and give you a better job in the future. The more education you have, the more knowledge you have.

Q. Is it wise to go on vacation alone? I am a female and recently finished college. I feel like going away for two weeks before I start a job. Please tell me if it is safe.

A. You can go on vacation to stay with a relation who can put you up for two weeks. You have not mentioned your age, though I can guess. If you are going with a friend or your family, it would have been safer and not lonesome.

Q. I am a young girl and very shy. I feel uncomfortable when I am among a lot of people. Can I overcome shyness?

A. Of course, it will wear off as you grow up. The more you advance in age; the young people around you will want to learn from your experience. You will also attain confidence to mix up with your mates.

Q. What is the best profession for a woman?

A. In the past, women were advised to be nurses or teachers. In this modern world, women can become whatever they want because everyone is having qualitative education.

TEENAGERS SPARE TIME

KEEPING BUSY

WRITING 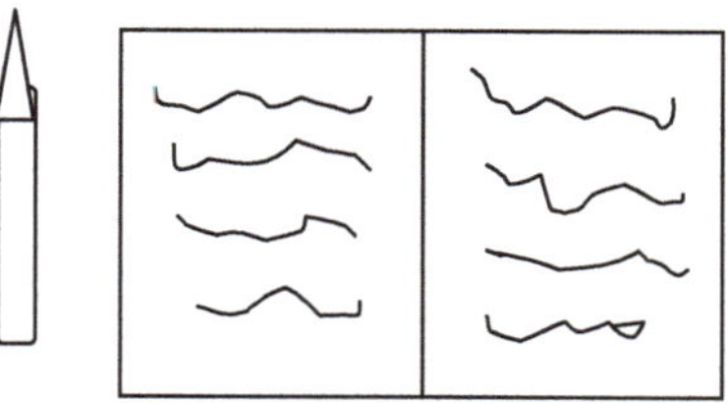

DRAWING 

PAINTING 

KNITTING 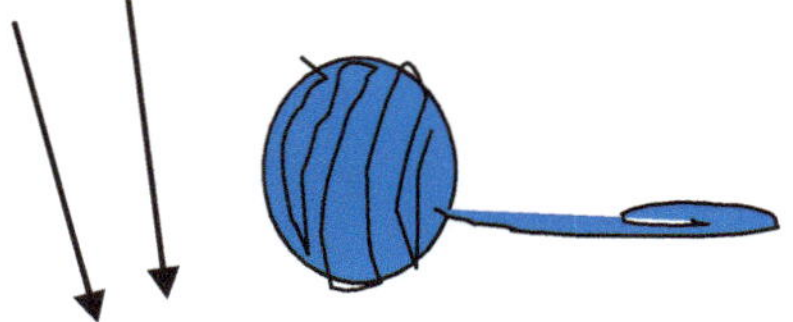

Purchase the cds by Jane Landey on Amazon music

Enjoy the first series of Mousse!

  Get it on Amazon.com

Young's Delight Magazine

Published by Brims World LLC

Young's Delight Magazine is a quarterly
magazine for youths. Subscribe for the
quarterly series in quarterly unit or yearly
bulk.

Send your address and subscription to the
following e-mail address:
brimworldincorp1@yahoo.com

Copy the following into your e-mail and
send.   ;

Name……………………………………………………………
…

Address………………………………………………………
…….

E-mail
address…………………………………………………..

Unit/Bulk……………………………………………………
…..

Once we receive your order, we will forward
it to your address and inform you through
your   e-mail address.